The Unpredicted Spring

Lockdown Poetry 2020

A Book Mill Publication

First published in 2020
by The Book Mill Press
Bongate Mill, Appleby, CA16 6UR
www.thebookmill.co.uk

Cover design © Neil Ferber
Cover Image © Hans Findling
Edited by Kathleen Jones
Selection and notes copyright © 2020 The Book Mill,
All rights reserved

Early March by Norman Nicholson © Irvine Hunt 2020

ISBN 978-1-9164750-4-5

Contents

Foreword

It has been a humbling and moving experience. The poems began arriving within three days of the Norman Nicholson Lockdown Poetry Competition being launched on July 8th 2020, and kept on coming, right up to the deadline on September 1st. We received over 230 poems from 129 poets, including entries from Canada, USA, Italy, Luxembourg, India, and Japan, as well as all parts of the UK.

These poems show that you can lock down many aspects of human life, but you can never lock down creativity, imagination, and the urge to communicate. The evidence bubbles through every page. From Maggie Wadey's bitter yet beautiful take on the challenges faced by 'A' level students, to the hope found by Susan Cartwright-Smith in the stems of a lavender plant, we are given privileged status to explore the most personal responses to the coronavirus pandemic of 2020.

It is highly appropriate that Norman Nicholson should be the inspiration for this competition and this book. Nicholson, who lived from 1914 to 1987 in the same house in Millom, Cumbria, knew all about lockdown. Diagnosed with tuberculosis in his late teens, he spent the best part of two years confined to a sanatorium, much of that under orders not to leave his room. Even after that, he had to protect his health for the rest of his life. Social distancing is something he would have recognised.

Congratulations to our winners – Martyn Halsall *(Learning Whimbrel)* in the Adult section and Katie Deutsch *(Silently Ignoring the World)* in the Under-18 competition. Congratulations too to the shortlisted poets: Flo Au *(He She It)*, Isobel Thrilling *(The Goats of Llandudno)*, Martin Rieser *(Wildwood)*, Rich David *(Ouzel)*, Marion Leeper *(What to Wear in Lockdown)*, Anne Banks *(One Walk a Day - Haiku)*, Kerry Darbishire *(In the Air)*, Nick Grant *(Demeter)*, Deborah Maccoby *(Violet Carpenter Bee)*, Rukshitha Arasakone *(Hidden)*, and Mehak Vijay Chawla *(Saviours Burning the Midnight Oil)*.

On behalf of the Norman Nicholson Society I thank Kathleen Jones most sincerely for her expertise and enthusiasm in first judging the entries and then putting together this wonderful anthology. Our thanks also to Neil Ferber for his design talents; the Book Mill for their outstanding generosity in publishing this anthology at cost price only; every poet who picked up a pen or set fingers to keypad and entered our competition; and Irvine Hunt, Nicholson's literary executor, for permission to print the World War Two poem *Early March*, from which our title is taken; 'The Unpredicted Spring' – it was certainly that. Not for the only time in his writing career, Nicholson came up with a poem which has more than stood the test of time.

I am confident that the poetry in this book will do the same.

Charlie Lambert

Chair, Norman Nicholson Society

Norman Nicholson

Early March

We did not expect this; we were not ready for this –
To find the unpredicted spring
Sprung open like a broken trap. The sky
Unfolds like an arum leaf; the bare
Trees unfurl like fronds of fern;
The birds are scattered along the air;
Celandines and cresses prick pinpoints white and yellow,
And the snow is stripped from the fells.
We were not prepared for this. We knew
That the avalanche of war breaks boundaries like birches,
That terror bursts round our roofs; we were aware
Of the soft cough of death in the waiting lungs. But this
Has caught us half-asleep. We had never thought of this.

Maggie Wadey

Like Swallows

They came like swallows, the young ones,
eighteen that year, beautiful, quarrelsome, absurd,
powered by desires as yet unspoken
and everything, everything, still to play for
even in their own doom-heavy, tech-laden, anxious times.

They came like swallows, the young ones, choosing
to win, to lose, to speak out, or some to keep
to the narrow path of personal ambition,
of love or study, holding faith that their future must surely deliver
something at least of pleasure, treasure, a measure
of the plenty lavished on their parents' generation.

They came like swallows, the young ones,
out of the traces and into the race,
torn as they were between fight or flight,
high-hearted even in this damaged place
that we, like careless thugs, have gifted them.

They came like swallows, the young ones, flying,
into the mockery of this year's spring.

2

Kerry Darbishire

In the Air

What if this should change?
The crab apple in blossom
leaning on a hawthorn like an old friend.
The brown and white cows cudding the lush meadow
beyond the wall. The rumble of John's tractor
checking ewes and lambs.
Tyres weaving morning's dew.
The hedge of May like brides in wedding gowns
beneath a lucky blue sky.
What if this should change?
These thistles pushing through turf
keen as fans at a football match. My dog,
nose to ground tracing every drop of last night's musk.
The resident owl who never seems to sleep
calling from the ghyll where the Plough always stops
between two sycamores and the smell of weather stays sharp.
What if this should change?
The first swallows leaping air at finding last year's nests
in the barn. Orange tips giddying bluebells by the river
playing last night's rain. The cheeky pair of squirrels
darting up the trunk of the pine. The cocky pheasant
parading his apple orchard.
What if this should change?
Bracken brushing green over the fell
where my children found bleached skulls
and the distant estuary gleams like a star, here,
where winter follows footprints through gorse,
where deer and fox graze unafraid.
What if I never hear their bark again?

Anne Rabbitt

Bookshelf Ballad

Breaking news
Offshore
The plague
Quarantine

Wilful disregard
We are all completely beside ourselves.
What do you care what other people think?
Someone like you

Border crossing
Complications
A death in the family
This changes everything

Born to win
Taking control -
For your own good
Missing out

Fatigue
Depression
Nausea
Days without end

Lost connections
Restless;
The cost of living.
The distance between us.

The worst-case scenario
The death of the family
Afterwards
Free fall.

H is for hawk
Heroes
Housekeeping
Happy ever after.

New lives, new landscapes
Guns, germs and steel
All the birds singing
Our common future

One hundred years of solitude
Skippy dies
Out of site
A crime in the neighbourhood

Isobel Thrilling

The Goats of Llandudno

Goats are eating the municipal flowers
in Llandudno,

they trot from plate to plate
of tulips,
primulas, violets
set out like iced cakes.

Here comes the light orchestra
of hooves,
occasional bray from a throat,
small blasts
from vocal accompaniment,
bleat-music.

And people locked up by the virus,
those who fashioned
the gardens
as stained-glass windows,
watch through panes,
as creatures devour a street-feast,

retreat
to the Great Orme at midnight,
to sleep off
the crimson, scarlet, purple and gold.

Katie Deutsch

Silently ignoring the world

It is late.
Scrolling through my phone
Silently
Ignoring the world

At this time
I can pretend nothing is wrong
Everything is normal
Everything is good

While the world is in shambles
I sit alone
In my room
It is late

Silently ignoring the world.

Marion Bowman

For Joan and George

4 June 2020

The rain swept over Bass Lake in a smoky pall
The day they burned your body.
It was the end of that parched, dry spring of
Twenty twenty –
Blurred visions of just how wrong we'd gone.
No rain, and ash trees dying back –
The cindery hints of where we were to go.
I watched the shower cloud
Swing round the peak of Lord's Seat
And Barf from high on Noble Knott
With Skiddaw wreathed in grey
And me in sorrow at your passing.
Binsey to the West,
The rain-sad fells indifferent to our follies,
Spattered by tearful drops, the downpour sweeping East
Through long, long empty glacial valleys.

It had been the hot, unseasonal spring of
Twenty twenty –
Blurred visions of just how wrong we'd gone.
Through visors, swathed in gloves and gowns,
The pestilence and plague that brought you down.
No sight of you those last weeks, isolated,
The virus taking hold and silencing your voice,
But, still, I heard a distanced call from you –
Make life matter.

We moved into the fervid Covid summer of
Twenty twenty –
Blurred visions of just how wrong we'd gone.
When all the meanings of 'I can't breathe'

Turned sharp and cleared the air,
And showed a path, the sunlit way you'd gone,
The way of love, and joy, and passion:

All life matters.
All lives matter.
Black Lives Matter.

Cathy Whittaker

Bad Corona Day

You want to sing your way to work,
hang round the photocopier chatting,
at lunchtime you want to go to Treacles
order quiche and coleslaw
say hi to the waitresses who know you,
you want to buy wine and chocolate
take it round to your friends,
you want to have a BBQ
go inside if it rains,
you want to browse the shopping centre
buy a new shirt or a scarf,
you want to pick up a book from Smiths,
read the first paragraph, sigh,
put it back on the shelf, find another one,
you want to ring your brother
ask him to stay over
wander the streets together, read menus, choose,
have a few drinks first in a pub,
you want to take a long drive
to see your daughter
you want to hug her and the children
take them out for treats,
shopping, beach days, picnics.
You want to see your friends in the coffee shop
drink iced tea
not worry about masks
and how long the virus hangs around,
you want to go to writing workshops
gather inspiration, meet new people,
go for long weekends on retreats,
now it's Zoom and nothing else
and its grief that hits you in the morning
when you have a bad day.

Philip Burton

Hard Boiled Covid Street

Newly wed, we plagued the council. They coughed up a house
made of highly fragrant paint, a room with rough enamel bath,
boiler in the scullery, a separate room for anthracite,
liquorice flooring. We were into each other, a *menage a trois*:
she, the house, the adolescent me.

Being innocent as two cherries, wild as weeds,
young as the walls and street, we danced on the ceiling, went ma
with stucco, rainbow kitsch, footprints in concrete, garden mirro
gnomes, wind chimes, and a mind-bending fence a child
could have painted and did.

Covid 19 zonked us, martyred our best bits,
put the old oven lid on the left field we'd planted.
The jazzy pagoda crackled and stained the communal bonfire.
Carnival was clammed shut in its own Pentonville.
Our dwelling surrendered to the street,

became humdrum, vanilla, cross-referenced to a week of Sunday
lawn yawning at the mower, nothing curtains, elephantine tv,
paint scheme white-with-a-ghost-of-tangerine.
Our house – one of a bag of hard boiled sweets stuck together.
Our bedroom – we've become wedded to it.

We've sugared our fudge and lie in it, toffee nosed.
We're waiters lying waiting, waiting for lockdown to end.
We moan down the figures, connect each new spike
with social-kiss-dancing neighbours who kick the new norm
to the end of the road where no mower mows.

Louise Mather

Prophecy

All the centuries   in the hollow
    of her palm   she held
        a dark feeling

    She had told him about
constellations adrift   the depths perplexed
   deep interwoven   mercurial emotions
   as if time grasped   laws   cold grief

A flicker of memory   unfolding
    a mass of smoke
   the boundaries   unblemished sky
bellowing blind furnaces   this underfoot

Spirals of petals   the price   unprepared
    she told herself   a fable
they calmed her   without truth   to contain it
in the box   with the blue rose
    slowly decaying   their absence
       we have made

She dreamt of   the night
morbidly   dread   with hands around
  her throat   the future   bare
    see-through tide
        a prophecy   of dust

No harbour for   worn wasted flesh
   a lustreless maid   to speak
    breaking coils of ash nebula
   shedding   sanguine   pools

11

She had mistaken
    fear   for   immortality
reason   embracing   insanity
    ignited   threefold

The sun   cascading beauty
    reclaimed
everything that came after   awaiting
    that she would lose everybody
      she had ever loved

The trajectory of exodus   scudding
    was she still on the floor
    he had told her   to stay
    away   to save us all
      Did it work?

Dick Smith

Hearing Them

No bull, nor finch, there!
soft fruit of sound
invites you not to hear;
not of the ground

not for last wide shore
of river to the sea,
not for sky-flayed moor; -
thumb-podded pea

pillowed in leaves? No, small
hinge cry for oil,
domestic love-knot call:
pearled private tell.

Martyn Halsall

Learning Whimbrel

He watched the birds by sound after his blindness,
calling to mind from hearing small cassettes
species from song; each voice, as experts phrased it.

He played tapes in the car, as fingering notes.
Historian, he never saw their geography.
Light was just dawn or dark, denying detail.

Lock on his eyes made prison, but also flight
as birds came, bringing in their ancient music
stories he'd once squint manuscripts to decode.

Tapes brought him gifts of fluency in recognition;
house martins' *trr, trr*, or *bier, bier* alarms
as harvesters scythed air; adobe nesters.

Locked down by plague, he'd conjure miles they travelled,
tartan migration, by flung songs that he'd heard;
sea-eagles' *krick-rick* poise, *ge ge* in soar.

His wife would check descriptions in her bird book,
kliep kliep in oystercatchers' black and white;
Lowlanders' *pluit* from an avocet.

Evening in islands, listening from memory,
her hand guided his elbow; his folding cane
probed track for boulder, he caught the lochan's music,

hearing *uid, uid, uid*, as Nordic phrasing
of whimbrel, mottled plumage like the burn
that flowed among the words she read to him.

Martin Rieser

The Window

I have been looking at this view for thirty years
dry-eyed or in tears, but now the sky seems bluer than before
and the trees more green – to one who hides indoors.

Outside remains the same, but in the air the virus flows
and must give pause to those who know the data and its flaws,
the sophistry of government and arbitrary laws.

Some call the dying by their names
and risk their all in simple acts, where kindness loses count
yet lifts the human from the mire, to balance the accounts.

Marion Leeper

What to wear in lockdown

Last night I dreamt
I went out into the street
wrapped in a long fur coat.

> People pointed. Shouted
> from doorways, windows.

They did not know that I was swaddled
in a hundred years of stories
to keep me safe from danger.

> They called out: 'A disgrace! An ugly woman
> Wearing the skins of beautiful animals.'

I said, it was a hundred years ago
my father wore rough fur
to line his coat, that Peking winter
when foreigners were locked down in their compounds
against the riots, sharing their meagre rice in bamboo rooms
and skating to keep warm.

> They remonstrated: 'Unprotected!
> In the street without a mask! You'll catch your death

I pulled the coat's round neck closer to mine, and said,
you do not know
how that long-forgotten lining
became a peace-offering between
my sister and my mother in their ten years' war
about clothes.

how my sister wrapped it round her, so the folds rippled
across her flanks, and her eyes
narrowed like a cat's.

Still they pointed: the coat waved behind me
a royal banner or a badge of shame.

I said, you've never seen how
those tawny markings, charcoal and umber,
particular as lifelines
spread over her bed, that winter
she spent alone, no money
in a stone-cold cottage with a too-small fire;
how, enveloped in a solitude of fur,
she read survival from their hieroglyphs.

Then I woke, remembering
that the coat had long ago gone to moth
and the streets were empty.

Rukshitha Arasakone

Hidden

Unbreathable
Untouchable
That's who we are.
We steal your identity,
Hoard oxygen.
But just like you,
We're created
In different sizes
A multitude of colours and shapes.
Some of us are thrown away,
Some kept by their owners,
Our mission in year 2020
Is to be everywhere, on everyone.
But aside from that
We save lives, stop the Covid.

Maggie Wadey

'How Do You Spell Apocalypse?'

"It was real hot for the time of year
and I remember thinking: '*If it's this hot here*
what'll it be like back home in Oz where it hasn't rained,
not so you'd notice, best part of a year?'
But we had the luck to be in London, city of our dreams,
and next April, 2020, was branded on my heart;
I'd be eighteen, my adult life would start.
Blissed-out on sunshine there in Parliament Square
we soon became aware some kind of demo was going on.
Encircled by police, a polite English crowd with pale bare arms,
sweet-faced girls and guys in tight black jeans,
was sitting in the middle of the road, waiting, an eternity it seemed
to be allowed to hand in letters to what I'd always supposed
was their very own House of Commons.
Then an old woman with bright blue eyes
lowered herself, groaning, to the floor beside us
and squinting at her notebook looked up to ask:
'*How do you spell apocalypse?*' "

Anne Banks

One Walk a Day – Haiku – March 2020

out on Cunswick Scar
curlews flute, skylarks warble
over silent roads

bright darts of sapphire
kingfishers shimmer upstream
spell of reflection

wood anemones
raise white faces to the sun
in golden limbo

garlic wild in woods
windblown beech splinters and falls
sirens on fellside

hawthorn leaves, new green
tremble in the frosted breeze
in town nothing stirs

woodpecker yaffles
wagtail, warbler, wren, take flight
planes grounded, skies clear

across grey stone walls
purple aubretia bellies
neighbours wave and chat

blossom by the Kent
gaudy branches reach towards
a padlocked playground

we keep our distance
shaken to see so many die
bluebells bow their heads

Rich David

Ouzel
(After Edward Thomas)

I remember Ouzel,
That afternoon,
Sitting by the river,
Watching the slow flow,
Of the water downstream.

It was May –
And a passing train thundered past
Every carriage empty.
Someone near coughed,
And we turned our heads,
Towards sunlit sky.

And for that second,
We could hear the faint
Murmur of song as
A murder of crows,
Flew higher and the whole world
Held its breath.

Pauline Yarwood

Secession

frauds! deceivers! you do not console
poetry's done for it's too hard now

yesterday I closed my eyes and saw
I was standing barefoot in darkness
facing the cavernous black opening
of a mountain tunnel I strained to pick up
the sound of a train which would surely
destroy me in seconds but no train came
what came was the thunderous cawing
and screaming of dark shapes that sped
towards me round me over me screeching
back-off back-off you stand alone
hundreds of them flying from black space
into black space hungry angry

they looked like ravens crows rooks
but I knew they were

words

Mike Smith

Cutting Firewood in a Heat Wave

I'm sawing old logs left to rot in next door's field
for years.

He's bored with wood-burning stoves.
Besides, it was only ever a game.

Dragged from the grass under hedgerow trees,
it's dried over time,

and now in this late May heat
is light as paper.

And the sawn lengths,
judged by hand and eye
to fit the stove's diagonal
at least,

lift like papyrus scrolls, I think.

Nothing in them though
to be saved for future generations;
nothing to be suppressed by flames.

I'll scatter their ash when the time comes,
at the feet of my apple trees.

Nick Grant

Apollo

God of the Sun, the Arts and Medicine

This is how you insulate from fear.

Rattling the little bottle into life

Each morning as a rite.

The right amount of water

In the same small coloured glass

And the right food before.

The safety cap pressed and twisted.

The unsaid incantation:

"Let this flow about me,

Inside,

This synthesis of health;

May the white coats flap about their work,

Precisely,

Diplomas from somewhere well reputed

Plastered on every wall,

Measuring out goodness for me

Confidently, paternally."

As far as I know this is witchcraft:

Trusting in someone else's artistry

Because it has been told of
So emphatically
And practised for so long.
A tightly folded paper
Tucked into every box
Gives it truth.
I'm not brave enough to disbelieve.
Give me the sun instead.

Mehak Vijay Chawla

Saviours burning the midnight oil.

Life was tattered and covered with grime,
many faced terrible difficulties all the time ,
shortages of food supplies and struggled for basic amenities.
Subhas Mahadik a posted man at Solid Waste Management,
after supervising garbage vehicles day and night,
became a patient of corona, refused by all hospitals,
while his condition deteriorated, and being depressed, citing unavailability of beds,
and died after two days of being admitted.
We should know he is our coronavirus warrior.
Managing funerals of loved ones who died of
corona became a struggling task,
Jitender Singh Shunty took it upon himself to perform the last rites of people,
conducted forty five incinerations and has been a saviour for the whole nation.
During Covid in Mumbai, Vijay Gite, a security guard,
burnt the midnight oil to make up the courage and do his job.
He wrote his experience on a trip to hospital, which pleaded citizens to stay at home,
at the last moment of his life, fighting with his wife to go to do his duty, but later he died.
What about the backbone of Brihanmumbai Municipal Corperation?
Ratnaprabha Dabholkar being a patient of diabetes and blood pressure,
always moved on and never lost her spirit to serve the country;
Dr Trupti Katdare was bombarded with stones by a mob in Indore;
they will unceasingly move on to serve the nation and perform their duties in these times.
Another female, Dr Zakiya Sayed, who got injured,
keeps on fighting and always has a hope to win in such a situation.
Battling hunger and fatigue, a labourer father with his seven-year-old son,
they trekked hundreds of kilometres in the heat bare-footed,
driven by the prospect of making ways to their abodes.
They were not alone, some had young children and pregnant women,
begging for food, screaming and roaring.
Physically challenged women, at the Chennai Corporation Centre, Nungambakkam,

worked through the night to prepare masks from reusable fabric,
for the sanitary health workers, contributing to the nation.
Asha workers were beaten to death for small protests,
going to conduct the door to door survey,
they knocked on a family's door, who refused to cooperate,
a family so mad that they blew their top, beating the Asha workers with sticks.
I feel proud of all these coronavirus warriors.
They struggled for the country's betterment and always had an optimism to help
So, why not help them by staying at home?

Fatima Anwar

Clap

For key workers working night and day
For hard workers at home
For self employed
For small businesses
For volunteering spirit

Clap
For school children
For efforts to home school
For sitting exams from home
For adapting to change

Clap
For exercising at home
For trying out new hobbies
For resisting meeting family
For group video calls
For phone calls
For smiling
For caring
For understanding

Clap
For patients fighting illness
For battling with mental health
For shielding
For elderly
For vulnerable

Clap
For following guidance
For sensible hand washing
For social distancing
For essential shopping

Clap
For this lockdown to end soon
Clap
For research to find a cure
Clap, clap, clap
For the world to be stronger
For the world to be at peace
For the world to be virus free.

Flo Au

He She It

Fill in the blanks with the words given.

It starts in _____ (China/ Italy/ France/ Germany/ Spain/ America…) and drowns boundaries to suffocate every healthy lung. It intensifies _____(apprehension/ arguments/ animosity/ anxiety…) among people of colors, same or different. To it, all _____(places/ colors/ ages/ genders…) are the same. No mercy on him. On her. On you. On me. Just it breeds and buds._____(Protests/ Tear gas/ Petrol bombs/ Gun shooting/ Ravings…) it fears not. It _____(lurks/ loiters/ plots/ snickers…) around the corner, fully armored in frequent, fatal ambushes over the frenzy for a vaccine. It has long existed in his, her, their and our world, some scientists say. Then why now? Why him? Why her? Why them?

The reporters say the sky is _____(cleaner/ clearer/ bluer/ brighter…) with wisps of bleach white, cotton clouds leisurely and joyously floating around. Rivers are _____(less smelly/ greasy/ trashy…), shimmering in light with ripples welcoming the dance of its fish woken from the dying state of slumber. Birds and insects of all kinds, unknown exotic species, in couples sing _____(more loudly/ sweetly/ touchy…) in the layers of green and red, yellow and orange, blue and purple. _____(Cows/ Sheep/ Boars/ Geese…) daringly leave their cramped habitats and stroll languidly along highways. It is different – the nature is back. What has _____(he/ she/ it) done? Sacrifices for prosperity Vs sacrifices for restoration of beauty? Who has the answer? Does he? Does she? Does it?

Deborah Maccoby

Violet Carpenter Bee: Spring 2020

A big black Bee against my window pane
Crackles with rage, struggling in vain
In wild frustrated agony to pass
The inexplicable barrier of glass.

The window's stuck. But I open wide
The big glass patio door, and guide
My winter tenant to the spring outside.

She circles once, then seems to hesitate –
Then sallies forth to feed and pollinate.
And I feel honoured to have set her free,
Essential worker for humanity.
When hierarchy breaks down in the hive,
Only the wild Bee keeps the world alive.

Carpenter Bee, brought to these northern climes
By a warming planet, in perilous times;
Violet Carpenter Bee, whose wings change hue
In sunlight to a dark translucent blue.

Wild flowers unfold for her their nectar treasure;
All nature wakes to labour that is pleasure;
Birds build their nests in budding trees and sing –
With gold-dust glistening on leg and wing,
From flower to flower my Bee goes visiting,
Oblivious to social distancing.

But while I set my Bee at large to roam,
Mankind immobilised remains at home.
A microbe holds humanity in thrall
Behind a baffling and invisible wall.

Lockdown will end one day, when they will find
A vaccine or a cure; but can mankind
Defeat the pathogen within the mind,
And, breaking man-made walls and distancing,
Experience at last the human spring?

Fiona Ritchie Walker

Distance

She wants to take these two hundred and twelve miles,
throw them in a hot wash,
shrink them,

turn these roads and fields into a screen,
watch her fingers
make them miniaturise.

If she could find a giant needle,
tack and gather north to south
she wouldn't care about the blisters.

In her mind, farm tracks buckle,
sheep popcorn as grass concertinas
small as a green scarf stuffed in her pocket,

church towers skew,
park benches shuffle
closer to each other,

the length of the country
cosies in, concentrating
at the snap of her fingers.

She won't mess with time,
that's what she wants, all the minutes
and hours in a true sharing,

so that when she rises from beneath
her own grey striped cotton,
bare feet take her

in two hundred and twelve steps
to sit at the oil cloth table
by the garden window,

pick a pear that yields
perfectly to her touch,
while he puts the kettle to boil.

Georgie Bailey

Little Moon

You seem so close,
yet so far away.
I wish I could pull this little me towards you
and lead myself astray.

Iain Twiddy

Flowers

In the midlands, the grind of the virus,
the concrete of lockdown, living the edge
of the wasteland not yet the new estate,

the sky as hard as the ground, as unlit
around the pounding silence of diggers,
breeze blocks, the stacks of stone, slapping wrapping,

surrounded by talk of shutdown and shutout,
collapse and depression and distancing,
the cage of contagion, herd immunity,

and the rumour – many-tongued as the blossom
still concealed in the trees – of the more death
the better, and pressure pressure pressure,

when the women emerge, late in the day,
take the air in their colours, three abreast,
big-bangled, each headscarf silken as wind,

and tender and slow share their thoughts,
one turns to laugh, in the key of me,
thin-stemmed and giddy, giggly as dawn,

planted once more with some long-buried sense
of how flowers work, what they do, how even
when the earth is disturbed, they make it through.

Aoife Mannix

Return

Last night you were suddenly burning again,
tipping your hands in the cool glass of water,
your cheeks flushed. This morning the air
is bright chill as frost glitters on the field,
patchwork crystals of a season
spun upside down. You say in your sleep
turn the light on, you don't know
where anything is. We are sealed
in our topsy turvy houses, trapped
by television, the fear of contagion.
Should I mark an X on the front door?
The children are putting rainbows
in the window. The muntjac deer
are back. Two of them slowly munching
the grass by the slide. Their small ears
twitching in the sunlight. I have never
been so glad to see them. Gentle creatures
from a very different spring. Wild wanderers,
still free and roaming through my mind.

Fatima Anwar

An unexpected guest

An unexpected guest arrived one morning
It came dressed in brightly coloured clothes and black shiny shoes
Laughing then crying
It wasn't too sure which emotion to choose.

This guest quickly got to know me
And we would laugh the night away
Sometimes we would cry rivers of tears
Those were the days I didn't want it to stay.

It was tricky at times to get to know this stranger
Sometimes we would be so silent-we wouldn't make a sound
Other times we would sing and dance
Stamping our feet on the ground.

On sunny days it would come dressed all in black
Even I would find that a little strange
We would sit indoors and eat all day
Then the next day it's clothes would change
To bright yellow and pink with a sparkly tie
We would be buzzing with excitement and talk to everyone
About our plans to conquer the world
And touch the bright blue sky.

Not many people understood this stranger
In fact many thought I had lost the plot
To accept something as peculiar as this
Who was in complete control of my thought.

I must admit it was hard for me too
To suddenly not know how you feel
Or who you really are
Sometimes my emotions felt too unreal.

But this stranger was now a part of me
It was with me through highs and lows
Changing the way I felt
As soon as it switched it's clothes.

Lately I've been suggesting what it should wear
It goes for a more casual look
With colours not too in your face
But sometimes it hates the idea of following a rule book.

An unexpected guest arrived one morning
Without any sort of warning
It chucked on a pink wig
And we both ended up doing a little jig.

Aoife Mannix

This Too Will Pass...

The quiet of the quarantined streets,
cars holding their breath,
the trees rustling in a breeze
made loud by absence.
No children on the swings,
just an old man walking his dog
past the closed shops. Their shutters
sighing with surprise. Even the hospital
is silent. One nurse with sanitiser
and a mask. A small nervous room,
a door where no one can be sure
they will come back. The doctor
in his blue apron, medieval
in his breathing. How fragile
this world we thought we knew,
how paper thin our history,
our technology, our security.
How much closer we are
to cholera, tuberculosis,
those old names we thought
we'd left behind. How much closer
we are to the truth of ourselves.

Martyn Halsall

The Inheritors

Never a father, he sired the inheritors
who follow him along green ways, and the old ways.
He leads them, like Moses, across the wilderness;
Norman Nicholson, poet of pebble and mountain.

He arrived early, sensing in the fiery furnace,
that lit the iron-works to an all-night sunset,
a smelting of warning. His lines were shod
with need to read a rescue for creation.

His tone, adagio; curlew over estuary,
shadow of Old Man mountain glimpsed from attic.
He transcribed singing stones, of lime and granite,
words his companions, to cast a summoning

to all children through whom flowed veins of ink,
to draft their protests as the weather changes,
following his footsteps where old nature of slag
restores itself in journals of this plague year.

He saw young, like himself, as refugees
from war, as he gasped shadows in the sanatorium;
as flying a box-kite into high, blue future,
as he sensed stirred world, breathing within his garret.

He taught them, green grandfather who saw beyond them,
casting his lines as angling for their futures;
calling them from his lock, beyond fells and walls,
to march, design red banners, defy by stanza,

to honour his grace-days, and re-cast his past
like his sculpted head, clear-eyed between hedging sideboards.
That staring into liberation after lock and key;
that miracle, turning a weather-vane into a pencil.

Martin Rieser

Wildwood

This is as close as the city gets to wild:
below the thunder of arterials, a blackbird thrills,
magpies clatter and complain, and a dog pauses
to listen, free from walls
and enclosed air, stale with traffic and fags.

Limestone spurs and gorges , grey-brown water,
stink of wild garlic, sheet-white frothing down the valley
and oaks, sentient oaks
standing their ground through season and storm,
their channelled bark, cicatrice worn
as skin, roots ravelling away into dark, touching
underground colonies, worm paths,
minerals and funghi; converting sunlight,
for the strong branches to cage the day-moon's face,
pushing slowly skywards.

They stand, every ring a ripple
out from the first shoot-
and our timespan barely girths an inch.

Martin Rieser

Leigh Woods in lockdown

Alone with blackbird and wren
under the leaves' arch
and beeches' green fire,
trunks sleek as unformed girls.

Distance on the city-
seldom cars rumble and hiss the Portway
civilisation sliding sideways
denaturing, diverging.

Dog-walkers edge past with tight smiles-
all a long way from home,
on a wide walk, eyes wary,
finding air in these airless times.

Pauline Yarwood

Things change

He'd have been over the moon, cock-a-hoop,
would've put his hands on my shoulders, held me still
and told me that I looked really good, so much better.
We never met without him asking why I always had my hair
so short. To deflect male interest? To punish him for not
seeing I was more than the way I looked? Because that first
love letter was addressed to the girl with short, short hair.
Because someone once said he couldn't believe he was
sleeping with someone with hair shorter than his,
and I deemed that a triumph.
Some of us have just Zoomed our oldest friend,
she's 89, the pale golden hair of her youth still with her,
and here on week 15 of lockdown our first conversation
is the one obsessing the nation – when will we dare get
our hair cut? One of us is cutting her own with nail scissors,
one of us, not yet embracing grey, colours hers at home,
one of us has cancelled the only appointment she could get,
one of us impulsively shot into an empty barber's shop.
We don't talk of the virus, we don't talk of Helen, Aphrodite, Isis
even of Samson, we know hair speaks, we know its power,
so Dad – look, at last, scared of dying I'm letting my hair grow.

Marion Leeper

Glimpses

The world's noise creeps back into the garden.
The thump of lorry on speed bump,
woodpecker builders, car park conversations,
while I am still peopling each corner
with stories to fill the silence.

Posting a letter at dusk
is a trip to another country,
the box's scarlet metal numinous with warning
and the yellow rectangle of a lamplit window
is a city where I do not belong.

Zoom-screen luring me in.
Hours, talking to pixels
except for that one dash across the street;
the prickle of rain on my neck
and the smell of fresh bread.

I had forgotten
mallow, alkanet, and evening primrose,
how footpath flowers, like children,
force colour through the grey stone
of our city lives.

Bats dash morse code across the garden twilight.
We talked of seas and swimming pools,
canal boats and cottages,
wartime deserts, childhood kitchens, death,
places we may not go.

My eyes are unused to far horizons;
wind farms, factories and railway tracks
jumble together into the chatter of a lark.
I mistake for builder's plastic that scarlet sea
of poppies picked out by fleeting sun.

 'I'm off to work,' you said,
shrugging on the fleece you've worn a million mornings.
The door's single clap, the bike tyre's crunch
and, left in silence, I wonder
when those sounds became so strange.

Susan Cartwright-Smith

Small Things

Small things, like a walk,

a leaf, a bird,

or a freckle shyly showing on a sun-kissed shoulder,

or an ammonite curling millipede,

discovered under lifted stone,

a snatch of tufted grass for nest in beak,

a grain of soil under fingernail

from long gone green-emerging fingers,

the fleeting smell of morning-dampened grass and woodsmoke,

                                  coffee fresh on stove, toast

and acrid tang of marmite

and the precious hour of time alone,

are punctuations to the endless days

where edges blur.

Anne Banks

Reading to Charlotte - June 2020

She tends to slip down out of sight,
I wonder if she has left,
bored by faun and beaver, lion and witch,
but then I spot the top of her head.
I hold up a picture, black and white,
she bobs up again, headphones
clamped on, eyes wide, laughing.

I want to reach through the screen
grab her hand tight and pull us both through;
run with her, race with the dryads and naiads
centaurs and leopards, follow
the great river downstream
to Cair Paravel by the shimmering sea .

I touch the glass...........

Nick Grant

Demeter

Goddess of the Harvest

This is labour.

Not the kind that called my grandfather

From bed to cold water to yard

Into the weak sun

Saying "I need two men, across the fields

And down the orchard path,

To mend the high fence" –

Driving piles all day into the soft and stony ground.

I could do that by habit, by need,

By my body seasoning each month

To suit necessity.

This, is the labour of care.

Nursing weeds from their uninvited clutch,

Finding the patch where the sun will stay

Longest and strongest,

Holding a tiny seed

Straggling with germination,

Pinching the damp earth close about a stalk,

Watering when there is none.

Goddess, this goes against my grain.

Not solving, not acting,

Not linking two unmet minds

With sly and unimpeachable

Language.

This is difficult for me.

Let me be tender and slow,

Willing to wait for bloom.

Georgie Bailey

The Wasp Nest

Watched the wasps all day,
flittering in and out, round and about.
Little shitty critters.
Bastards of the Universe –
history's hated atrocity with a stinger.
Had a book full of to-do's, but
filled my time instead, the only way I knew;
stood at the crack in the spare room window.

Against a hydrangea backdrop,
in their black and yellow fuzz;
perfectly structured stripes
and love-laced wings no bigger than a q-tip;
they duck, dive, weave and surround and
I watch, astounded. I revel. I marvel.
All through the crack in the spare room window.

And I wonder why I'm attracted
to the things that will hurt me the most,
and with no apparent reason.
And although I worship the sight,
I'll only admire from a distance,
like a toddler, gazing at their first kite flying high.
For now, I'll stick to my space, them to theirs;
stung one too many times, perhaps.
Goggling, gazing, gawping. All from the delicate bubble
I create. From the space dividing me and them;
appreciating the slither of life I can see
from the crack in the spare room window.

Mike Smith

Curtain Call

I'm not in the next scene.

I'm not on stage,
but lingering in the wings
(where I can see the ropes and wires
behind the back-scene flats).

The script has dropped me
from this page to the last.
Blame the director for my moves,
and the writer. I took my cues from him.

I neither nod nor walk on till the end,
when we take hands to make our curtain call
and see the audience clap and rave
or hear them shuffle, silent, from the hall.

Too late now for re-writes, edits;
for tweaking costumes,
devising bits of business,
new marks on which to stand;
adjusting lines of sight
(giving notes to younger members of the cast,
controlling prima-donnas, divas, at the last).

Some lighting engineer beyond the Gods,
to win a bet he made with someone from the pit,
has swung a spotlight side to side
and swept the hero from his mark
just for a lark.

Outside, the fans are gathering at a door.
I'll shoulder through unseen.
No-one will call my name.
That's a relief,
considering the character I've been.

Susan Cartwright-Smith

Emerging

I am two metres from the only other person
who is with me on our walk,
which feels rebellious
or somehow
dangerous,
as we are now unsure
if what we do,
a simple act of walking,
is allowed.
But while we agonised
and stood apart
and stayed alone and masked
and watched the clear blue skies
and heard the birdsong,
life went on.
And greenery has claimed the barren earth,
and flying insects flit amongst the dancing stems.
And in the water alien creatures
metamorphose undisturbed
by net or plastic tub.
And everywhere is full of life, and verdant
in this lost words world
which I have found once more.
And me, and my walking partner,
two metres behind me
find that life,
which finds a way,
continues undisturbed,
welcoming back those who gently tread,
emerging slowly,

like a nymph,
becoming other in a new world.
Behind our masks,
feeling somehow lost,
but finding ourselves once more,
we find the words
to say
this world
is beautiful.

Susan Cartwright-Smith

Renewal

Scraping back dead comfrey
revealed a crumbling legacy
and ampersanding worms
whose naked flesh surprised us all,
and clipping back the rosemary
let cowslips dance
and Easter roses gaze to heaven.
I hack into woody stems of lavender
sprawled like weathered legs
across emerging peony puckered lips
and pick the stems of life,
and with an eye to next year
plunge them into waiting earth.
Hope, a green fingered goddess,
looking onward.

Acknowledgements

Thanks must go to the Norman Nicholson Society for creating this project and to Charlie Lambert for all the hard admin work involved in organising a poetry competition. Thanks also to the Estate of Norman Nicholson and David Higham Associates for permission to include Norman Nicholson's poem 'Early March'. To Neil Ferber for the cover design and typesetting, and Hans Findling for the photo. A big thank you to all the poets who allowed their work to be included in the anthology, whose proceeds go to fund the work of the Norman Nicholson Society. More details of the Society can be found at https://www.normannicholson.org/

Brief Biographies

Fatima Anwar is a pharmacist in the vibrant, colourful and culturally diverse city of Glasgow in Scotland. Over the years she has grown to love writing and reading poetry as it provides a platform to channel her thoughts and raise awareness of different issues such as common misconceptions within society. She also uses poetry to highlight the striking beauty and character of nature and the effect certain human activities can have on the environment.

Rukshitha Arasakone has just turned 14 years old. She goes to the West Kirby Grammar School and loves it. She has many talents such as singing, dancing, and playing the piano. In English, she loves writing narratives and descriptions, but also likes writing poems. Her nationality is Dutch and she lives in the Wirral.

Flo Au won the Most Creative Award in Hong Kong's Top Story 2015. Her pieces are published in literary journals like *Aaduna, Pif Magazine, Star 82 Review, Gravel Magazine, Quarterly Literary Review of Singapore, Peacock Journal* and *Flash Fiction Magazine*. Her work was nominated for Best Small Fictions 2019, Best of the Net 2019 and Pushcart Prize 2019.

Georgie Bailey is a working-class Poet, Playwright and Producer originally from Bordon, Hampshire, currently living in Bristol. He is a recent graduate of Bristol Old Vic Theatre School's Dramatic Writing MA alongside being an alumnus of several development schemes such as Soho Theatre and HighTide Theatre's Writer's Labs. Georgie is also a mentor of new writers through creative projects at venues such as the Lion and Unicorn Theatre, London Playwright's Workshop and Chichester Festival Theatre.

Anne Banks lives in Kendal and is a member of creative writing groups Brewery Poets and Writers' Rump. She has recently had poems published in *Orbis* journal and the anthology *This Place We Know*. Anne is currently working on a poetry 'diary' of 2020, 'One Walk a Day was written in March/April and the first one written in lockdown, 'Reading to Charlotte'was written in June.

Marion Bowman is a Maryport girl originally, and with deep roots in Cumbria, the Borders and Northern Ireland, Marion Bowman now lives in Cockermouth after a career in journalism and broadcasting in London. As chair of the charity Kirkgate

Philip Burton has been a Lancashire head teacher and a poetry practitioner for children. In 2019 he concurrently held four poetry competition First prizes, including Sandwich (Kent) Poet of the Year. Philip was recently awarded a Commendation by Heidi Williamson in the 2020 Poetry Society Stanza competition. His poetry publications include *The Raven's Diary* (joe publish 1998), *Couples* (Clitheroe Books Press 2008), *His Usual Theft,* (Indigo Dreams Press 2017) and *Gaia Warnings* (Palewell Press 2021).

Susan Cartwright-Smith is a writer and artist who takes inspiration from the wild waters and windswept landscape of Cumbria. She is a wild swimmer and fell walker, and writer in residence for Cumbria Wildlife Trust's Gosling Sike site in Carlisle. She is a member of Carlisle Writers' Group, and one of the Caldew Press small press team.

Mehak Vijay Chawla is a fourteen-year-old girl studying in freshman year of high school from Delhi, India. Her source of inspiration for writing poems and short stories is the young diarist Anne Frank. Christopher Mudgett, an American Artist, is the one who inspires her to enrich her creativity in drawing and painting. She has just learnt one thing in life and that is to give everything she has, to her passion and academics.

Kerry Darbishire lives in Cumbria, England where most of her poetry is rooted. Her two poetry collections: *A Lift of Wings* and *Distance Sweet on my Tongue* are with Indigo Dreams Publishing and a biography, *Kay's Ark* with Handstand Press. Her poems appear widely in magazines and anthologies. She has won and been shortlisted in several prizes including Bridport 2017. Kerry is currently working on pamphlets and a third collection.

Katie Deutsch was born in northern California in 2006. She lived there for ten years before moving to England. She is now in year ten at a school just outside Cambridge. She lives with her parents and two siblings and is very fond of searching through old bookstores, and she enjoys what she finds there.

Rich David is a writer and musician from Northamptonshire. Since graduating from The University of Buckingham, he has worked as an English lecturer. He has released two albums with The Reeds, Let This Begin (2013) and Another Place (2018), and a solo album, The End of East Street (2020). He is currently working on his debut novel and his first collection of poetry.

Nick Grant lives in south west London with his family. He's a lawyer now but has been writing poetry since his teens. Lockdown disrupted his usual daily commute-work-commute rhythm and opened up a new opportunity for personal reflection. The two poems in this anthology are taken from a series of "prayers" to redundant gods that use the form of a one-sided plea for help or guidance in trying to voice the insecurities of our current trauma.

Martyn Halsall trained as a teacher, which led him into journalism. After reporting for local and regional papers, he joined *The Guardian* as a staff correspondent. His poetry publications include *Sanctuary* (Canterbury Press), reflecting on his year as the first Poet in Residence at Carlisle Cathedral, and *Visible Music* (Caldew Press) about experiencing cancer. He has also published five pamphlet collections, and lives and writes near Holmrook in rural West Cumbria.

Marion Leeper is a poet and purveyor of stories and tall tales based in Cambridge, UK. She fell into poetry when she was elected Bard of Cambridge for a year and has been happily drowning ever since. She has written on storytelling in education, and toured storytelling shows around the UK and beyond. Her poems have appeared in anthologies including *The Fenland Reed* and *In Other Words* for Allographic Press.

Deborah Maccoby gained an M.Litt degree at Oxford for a thesis on the poetry of Emily Brontë (after a BA in English Language and Literature, also at Oxford). Her literary biography of the Anglo-Jewish First World War poet Isaac Rosenberg – *God Made Blind* (Symposium Press) – was published in 2000. Deborah worked at the BBC World Service until taking voluntary redundancy/early retirement in 2008. She lives in Leeds, where she moved from London in 2015.

Aoife Mannix has published four collections of poetry and a novel. She has previously been poet in residence for the Royal Shakespeare Company, the Portsmouth Museum and BBC Radio 4's Saturday Live amongst others. She has a PhD in creative writing from Goldsmiths, University of London. She is originally from Dublin but now lives in the Cotswolds just outside of Banbury. www.aoifemannix.co.uk @aoifemannix – twitter

Louise Mather is a writer and poet from Northern England. She lives in a village in West Lancashire with her partner, son and cats. Her work is published or upcoming in *Streetcake Magazine, The Cabinet of Heed, Versification, Crow & Cross Keys* and *Idle Ink*. She is currently working on her first collection.

Anne Rabbitt is a writer/performer whose work includes TV, film, theatre, comedy and prose. She has been long & shortlisted for several writing competitions. She grew up in Manchester, studied Dance & Art at Goldsmiths and received a distinction from Birkbeck in Creative Writing (MA). Her short film, *Bookshelf Ballad* (4 stars The Scotsman), was shown online @theSpaceUK in lieu of her solo show at The Edinburgh Festival 2020 and can be seen on YouTube.

Martin Rieser is a poet/artist from Bristol and two of the poems refer to Leigh Woods – an ancient woodland wild space just across the Clifton Suspension Bridge which is one of the city's "lungs" and was his only accessible space by foot, of this kind, during the spring lockdown.

Dick Smith lives in Kents Bank. He's also lived in Kendal and Grizebeck. Born into farming, he now keeps 20 odd hives of bees and 3 odd hens. He writes verse when forced to. Current projects: date-titled lyrics, aiming (it's a race; the force is fickle) to cover 365 - working titles: Momentary Calendar, Yakker's Almanac – and a Life in ottava rima addressed to his grandchildren (one of the eight might read it).

Mike Smith has written poetry, plays, short stories (as Brindley Hallam Dennis) and essays (mostly on the short story form and on adaptation). His writing has been published, broadcast and performed here, there, and elsewhere. He lives on the edge of England.

Isobel Thrilling was brought up in a mining village on the North York Moors, read English at Hull University, and has been published in many anthologies, magazines, (e.g. *The Observer, The New Statesman*), broadcast on ITV Country Calendar, BBC TV, Radio 3 and 4 and has won many prizes including first prizes at Bridport, Kent/Sussex, Stroud and second prize at York. Her poems have been set for GCSE English and she has five collections, the latest being *Close Encounters*.

Iain Twiddy studied literature at university and lived for several years in northern Japan. His poetry has appeared in The *Poetry Review, Poetry Ireland Review, Stand, The Stinging Fly, The London Magazine, Harvard Review,* and elsewhere.

Maggie Wadey is a screenwriter for television and also a novelist. Her last book was a memoir of her mother and Ireland, 'The English Daughter' (Sandstone Press, 2016). Poetry is a recent undertaking, but in September she had the remarkable experience of having a poem, 'Like Swallows' read out at a huge XR demonstration in Parliament Square. She lives with her husband, an actor, in Hackney.

Fiona Ritchie Walker is originally from Montrose in Angus, but has lived in NE England for many years. She writes poetry and short fiction, which has been widely published in collections, anthologies and magazines. She has an MA in Writing Poetry from Newcastle University.

Cathy Whittaker has a sequence of 15 poems published in *Quintet,* Cinnamon Press. Her poems have appeared in *Under the Radar, Prole, The Interpreters House, Envoi, Orbis, Southlight, Obsessed with Pipework, Mslexia,* and other magazines. She was shortlisted for the Bridport Prize. She was published in, *This Place I Know: A New Anthology of Cumbrian Poetry,* Handstand Press. Her poems based on her childhood in the lakes were longlisted in Frosted Fire Firsts, Cheltenham Poetry Festival and also commended in the Geoff Stevens Memorial Poetry Prize, Indigo Dreams.

Pauline Yarwood is a poet and potter living at Starnthwaite, just outside Crosthwaite, in Cumbria. She is the co-ordinator of Brewery Poets in Kendal and co-founder of the Kendal Poetry Festival. Her work has appeared in *The North, Strix, The Interpreter's House* and several anthologies. Her debut pamphlet, *Image Junkie,* was published by Wayleave Press in 2017.

Lightning Source UK Ltd.
Milton Keynes UK
UKHW020736040121
376219UK00005B/36